All poems © Adam Lowe, 2009. All rights reserved.

This collection of poetry is designed to highlight the work of a local writer. Please share it with your friends and consider contacting the author at adam@adam-lowe.com for further information or additional copies.

Adam Lowe also runs workshops and editorial services for writers. Please contact him for rates and further information. His first novel, *Troglodyte Rose*, is available from Cadaverine Publications in limited hardback from 30th October 2009 and in trade paperback from CROSSING CHAOS enigmatic ink in spring 2010. Check out the website at troglodyterose.com.

A Fruit Bruise Press collection.

Fruit Bruise Press
(A division of Dog Horn Publishing)
6 Athlone Terrace
Armley
Leeds
LS12 1UA
United Kingdom

Paperback edition: 978-1-907133-10-7

Fag Mouth, Fag Tongue

FRUIT

You call me a fruit,
and I agree,
say

a fruit is ripe,
promising seeds,
bursting with juice.

You call me a fruit,
as though a vegetable
and I list a litany
of fresh attributes:

a fruit is rich,
remembers its roots,
nourishes, quenches,
makes a display of any table.

I say,
I am the apple
that announces the gravity
of a given situation;
I am the pomegranate
that teaches of possession;

I am the fig
our ancestors couldn't resist.

You call me a fruit
and I agree:
soft, round and sweet.
I dare you to peel back my layers,
take a look at my pips.
Full as a watermelon,
sharp as a lime,
come over here
and bite me.

COLLECTING

As he walks
down the bitter
winter high street
fag boy collects
the shrapnel
of dirty words
thrown his way

gathers
in his travel bag
a queen
a poof
a faggot

a pussy
he didn't even
know he had

he totes
this bag of tricks
shards jingling
back
to his apartment
and there

with patience
assembles
his assortment
of dirty words
those hurting words
and fashions together
a queer poem

PRIDE

If I wanted
to be thinner
I'd skip dinner
shackle
my limbs
to a treadmill

If I wanted
to be bigger
a weightlifter
I'd lift cars
pull bars
and fight

If I wanted
your approval
I'd demand it
never ask
always
assured

If I wanted
to be patronised
I'd be quiet

close my eyes
and beg
on all fours

Instead
I stand here
resilient
and complete
and brush
the droplets
of your
disapproval
from my back

THE BODY ISSUE

He slithers
through my door
sheathed
in cellophane
and there he lies
    naked
        rippling

his smile
whiter than
polar bears
in sunlight
his tanned
English skin
darker even
than the Carib
in my genes

he's glossy
and shimmering
made of nothing
but paper

the perfect

beloved
indeed

THE OFFER

Fag boy declines
your offer
to take part
in society

instead he turns
his back on
      government
      police and
      money

he'll sit at home
write a poem
roll over in
his bed

he'll hike up hills
and sleep in caves
knead and bake
his own bread

fag boy sees
the snares you lay
the world with which

you trap

    he wants to write
        he wants to sing
            he wants to kick back

SAFER SEX

I've noticed,
as a gay man
sex is never safe,
only safer,
because we take it up the anus.

Our blood
is contagious,
from a life of sin.

Our skin
is porous and leaking,
so I should be masked
and gloved before we even greet.

It seems
even if we slip,
we damn ourselves,
whilst heteros fuck
ungloved, carefree and innocent
at whim.

NOTE TO SELF

Remember:

Virgins
of a certain age
lack experience
for a reason.

Gossip
might be malicious but
it also might be true.

Secrets
undo friendships
faster than loose ropes
and winds undo sails.

Poetry
scares off boyfriends
like herpes on your face.

I Wrote You a Letter . . .

TOOTHBRUSH

You gulp down the last of the orange juice,
full of sunshine glow like an advert.
Or maybe it's just me that sees it that way,
like we're in California
and not the windy north of Britain.

I follow as you climb
barefoot up white-painted stairs,
lit by the lightbulb
against the spangling of stars above
through the skylight.

The bathroom sparkles,
citrus and blue,
and the extractor fan whooshes a muted applause
broken only by the click
of a flipped toothpaste lid.

You smile at me,
telling me about your new boyfriend,
whilst polishing your Hollywood teeth.
I hold the basin for support,
tipsier than I'd thought,
and stare at the Colgate on the side.

When you go to bed
I stare at white foam splashes
sliding slowly towards the plughole,
and hopefully, achingly,
I push our toothbrushes together.

BREAKING OVER BREAKFAST

I want to cook you breakfast
I want to make your tea
stay a while longer and
lie here beside me

I want to feed you chocolates
I want to peel your grapes
and if you stay beside me
I promise not to beg

so stay a while longer here
let's talk
let's kiss
let's play
so stay a while longer here
until your wife awakes

PERMISSION

I never asked you
to come here
I never asked you
to stay
you came to sleep
beside me
and never went away

STONES

I may be carrying
stones dug by others,
men not you
but once beloved.

Their names come runny,
as blood, not spunk,
like Paul, Peter and Mike.

Forgive me if
I weigh too much,
am heavy
as I lay above you.
The weight is theirs,
I need to shed it,
before you turn cold
and blue.

STETHOSCOPE

I place the silver cup to your ribs,
as though listening to a hill
for the march of enemies approaching.

I hear nothing,
but smell dahlias and know them
to be the smell of your fear.

VALUE OF X

I remember
riding in the front seat of his car.

I remember
fish and chips with his parents,
two dogs, half-crazed,
padding and panting from kitchen to sitting room
and back.

I remember
your dream of becoming
a fireman,
which promptly turned to smoke
after we broke up.

I remember
when I still dreamed
of a life for two,
not yet frozen and perennially
hopeful.

But what is the value
of looking back?
If I remember,

can I ever be satisfied
with simply remembering?
Or will I,
fumbling backward for a prior life,
never move on?

From what do I subtract
to make one?
Or does me minus you
equal nought?

Post-Cocaethanol Blues

WAITING BETWEEN TRAINS

Waiting between trains
at Leeds station,
I see boys cup
the lower backs
of girls they want to own.
I see fathers
hoist children
onto broad, arthritic shoulders;
listless ravers
dressed in *de rigeur* pirate boots,
dubstep blaring out their headphones,
faces sagging with
post-cocaethanol blues.

The tickets in my hand
have become spent signs
warning of my departure,
reminding me of you.

And it seems to me,
at these portals,
where multiple jostling
finite worlds pour and seep together,
the universe is moving,

like the shifting faces of
a Rubik's cube,
while I,
with all this baggage,
always waiting,
stand still.

SHRUNK

She told me
I had a broad emotional range;
that my kindness is often mistaken
for naivety in strangers;
that I revel in being loved,
but grow bored when engaged.

I chortled with mirth.
I swaggered with rage.
Puffing up with pride,
I took centre-stage.

I met a new man,
looked gleeful into his eyes;
and when he looked back,
his eyes turned to mirrors,
and with a shiver, I grew cold
inside.

INTO THE WOODS

You've done this before,
I think, as you lead me through the poplars,
we negotiating moss and fallen twigs,
like post–Blitz debris.

You love your boyfriend,
you admit with fatigue,
but this is different,
you say, back against the breeze.

There's a scurrying
of wildlife on the ground,
a rabbit or a squirrel,
but I wonder if maybe,
tunnelling through forest floor–down,
I can smell a rat
with bubonic fleas.

You kiss me on the neck,
then get down to your knees,
taking me in
with porn star expertise.

Overhead a leaf turned brown

curls down from the thatchwork canopy,
landing in your hair.
I brush it away,
see, in your eyes,
an eagerness to please.

I don't care how he feels,
the man who waits alone
on an Ikea sofa;
I just wish this snatched moment,
would satisfy my needs.

THE TEA PARTY

I enter the toilet,
to see you sat on the lid.
This, our cottage,
done up today in doilies.
On the edge of the sink,
rests fine blue china,
a teapot, two cups,
a saucer, arranged round
the rim.

Your wig is tilted,
which I pretend to ignore,
as you right the illusion
with a lacquered paw.

You pour sickly stinking
gloriously dark Darjeeling,
the colour of molasses,
and just as sweet.
Steam rises,
to veil your face in secret,
forbidden femininity.

I neaten the hankie

in my blazer pocket.
Sipping my tea,
I realise I'm staring
past the gently cracking
overdone mascara,
into your wanting
hazelnut eyes.
I crack a smile
to match
and play along with
your lies.

THE PRICE OF INFLATION

I did it for TV,
an article on extreme male beauty.
It seemed like
the perfect opportunity—
a bigger cock to show off
and my fifteen minutes of fame.

Perhaps if I wasn't
so vain, I'd have said
no. Told them
where to go.

For a moment
I hesitated,
decided not to proceed.
My editor reminded me,
it was an operation
I really didn't need.
But I got a call
from the producer,
who upped my fee,
reminded me it was only for a year,
said he'd put my name forward
to be a presenter for the BBC.

Naturally, I was elated,
and when I saw my cock inflating,
half-delirious through their drugs,
I was anxious to display
my brand new designer dick.

It isn't a trick, I'd say.
From eight inch to twelve!
Buy now,
get fifty percent extra
free. A limited
time only.

But then came the hard part.
No sex for a month,
or at least three weeks.
Loose boxers mandatory,
to avoid restriction
and the forming of lumps.
(Imagine my dismay
to think of my prick
swollen and uneven like
poorly-made gravy.)

For the first few weeks,

I showed it off.
Flashed it at parties,
let strangers caress it
like Sir Walter Raleigh
returned from sea
with some shiny new fruit.

Sex was an impracticality.
A tearing of peach flesh
from around the pit core.
Every man was left sore.

Bored, I wished it would
dissipate sooner,
return the Titanic
to an elegant schooner.

But it taught me compromise,
to bend over and let in the new.
And slowly my nympho mind
drew away to other things.
I rediscovered poetry,
and the tenderness of love,
although I had to invest
in Kingsize Durex,
which fit like a glove.

And now that it's gone,
leaving me natural,
I find myself prouder,
happier and more rounded.

So if I offer to show you
my humble dick,
I'll do it with pleasure.
I'll show off the smoothness,
the more suitable measure.
Just count yourself lucky
that this time it fits.

CINEMA

It started
when I saw you
lay your head on his shoulder,
two seats down
at the cinema.
The way your skull fit,
a fleshy key into the curve
between neck and arm,
as though parts from a model kit
on the same sprue.
Made me think
maybe I could fit too.

So when you smiled at me,
in the courtyard,
I hatched my plan.

Do you have a cigarette?
But of course,
I don't smoke.

You reached out,
fag in hand,
and I brushed your fingertips

as I took the Marlboro.
Fumbling to ignite it
on your lighter,
you must have known the truth.
This was all just a ruse.

That was three weeks ago,
and now you lie
      in my arms,
         to your boyfriend.
The pieces have been reorganised.
Your head locked
against my shoulder,
your breath washing
against my throat.

I've got what I want.

There's dried semen like glue
holding us together,
yet I can't help but feel
strangely disassembled.

DRAG

As I slide my feet
into vinyl,
six-inch killer heels,
I feel like Cinderella
stepping into
a glass slipper.

I feel my broad, brown
flat feet shrink
to elegant porpoise flippers,
and my manliness
contained by a rubbery seal skin.

Dressing myself
is like sealing my hard edges
into a sequence of shells,
where the flesh inside
softens to mollusc.

Spiralling keratin cups my pecs,
filling them out
as a shiny smooth clam
swallows my sex.

And at the last,
the wig I wear
is a deep sea sponge
carefully anchored to my head.

Cotton Songs

ISLAND EASY

It's not easy
living inland
when your bones singsong of the shore.

It's not easy
walking on tarmac,
when your flat feet yearn
to dance on palm leaves,
traverse sandy treads,
flipper in surf-ridden tides.
And inside, in your chest,
a heart beats pirate ship drums,
wanting free of an empire
whose ships beat with slave throes.

It's not easy
standing on an inner-city balcony,
dreaming of the plank and diving overboard;
or standing beneath telephone poles,
reaching tired hands towards claws made of bananas,
hoping for a handshake,
but deprived of fruit.

It's not easy

scouring an island for sunshine,
wanting the warmth,
but finding only cold.

BIG MAMA

Big mama
sing her song
her body
holy dome

she know how
        to make home
        bake dough
        spread toe

But big mama
can hold her own
when old man strike
she beat him back
till he left her alone

Now she sing
louder than before
her child snug safe
between teet and elbow

GARDEN

I plant your garden
full of rose
smile
and guard your home

You trust me
say I'm not like
those other niggers
but don't figure
how my rage
grow like chiggers
between my toes

See
when I plant rose
it's a net I grow
black thorns
ready to claw

and when I
watch your house
silent as a mouse
the rat in me
cunning

plans how best
to burn it down

PLANTATION

I planted the corpse
in Massa's garden,
to see if a slave
could bear fruit.

I watered, fertilised,
and hoed the land
that hated him,
while waiting
patiently
for blossoms.

He spreads roots,
in need of some,
crossing map lines;
reaching, I guess,
back home.

And when the roots burst
through soil,
I could see they were iron
chains, growing from his feet

In spring his head

was a cloud of cotton,
and slowly,
through to summer,
his bones, grown massive,
yawned into
a branching corona.

Birds nested in his arms,
children sat
on his shoulders,
and ghosts clung
to the rungs
of his frame.

He never bore leaves,
instead telling a story
through silence:
witness of a history
best forgotten.

SAFARI

Let me take you on safari;
let me show you the world.

See the gold
melting in the sunlight,
food for a thousand fools.

See here diamonds
the colour of blood,
filtering like a prism
the greed of men.

See the dead
rotting in ditches,
riddled with bullets
sold by American entrepreneurs.

See the riverbeds,
dried tearducts,
where dust lies undisturbed
for months.

See the elephant
on his side,

stripped of his tusks,
lying in a puddle
of darkened intestines.

See the tourists
in their jeep,
photographing lions,
unaware
of the hyenas at their heels.

SNAKE

You
a snake
man

slither
on your belly
hiss
if you can

Want
to break
man
and cheat
man
and fill
your greedy
palm

But I
stay calm
see you
in the grass
winding
cross my land

I got
a trap
man

will kill you
with me
bare hands

You
a snake
man

slide away
as fast
as you can

Dark House

ON THE KITCHEN FLOOR

Purpling flesh
slowly renders down to jelly
in the larder.
Her eyes
are the dead, pearly buttons
of fish at market.

Her hair splayed
across face and floor,
an extension of
the death rattle
to pour tangling from her mouth.

The grapes around her throat,
a bruised choker;
the depressed plum wristlets
marking her resistance.

I miss her,
and already the aga's chill
jostles painfully against
memories of before.

And there,

mere inches from her hand,
is a knife:
> clean;
> useless but
> reached for.

The cellar door yawns,
cold and disinterested,
but I remain listless:
a witness
to it all.

VALENTINE '09

Bluing underwater,
a nymph
or maybe a Hindu god,
I stand over you, composting,
turning reason to sludge.

Why did you set yourself
timeless,
a deep daguerreotype
is prismatic wet?
Were you searching
for Atlantis, or a mermaid
to love you?

Were you listening
with too much intent
to the waves' sonata,
or the sighing shifting
of the sand?

Bluing underwater,
a nymph or Hindu god,
I wonder if like Krishna
you'll return

to the world of man.

GRAVEROBBER

A sleazy mist slithers low
over tombstones;
a white owl hoots
in the shade.

I carry my spade:
a wooden cross
rooted to a metal heart;
an instrument of love;
a weapon.

And as I count
the graves, alone,
full of sorrow,
I remember
the way he turned
his head, his eyes
casting their focus
over me.

I stop,
stoop down,
bent-backed,
skin slack

with age.

his grave,
green with moss;
the words
bare whispers
on granite.

Time has not
been kind to us;
has weathered
all subtlety
away.

Falling to my knees
in praise,
I wipe my face,
lift my head
to the sky,
and mouth his name;

recall
his touch,
his kiss,
his presence.

I run fingers
through grass
as though
it were his hair,
and I tear loose
a fistful
of earth.

With my shovel
I dig;
I turn over soil.
I sweat
and toil
and moan.

I hit wood below—

a coffin.

There he is:
asleep
inside,
a rose caught
in winter's ice.

Frantic,

I reach down,
pull the lid
from the ground,
and gaze
at my love.

There he is,
rendered gothic;
beauty laid out
skeletal.

As I touch him
I shiver,
a necromancer,
and yearn
to turn to bone
myself.